EXPLORING THE WORLD

DE SOTO

Hernando de Soto
Explores the Southeast

BY ANN HEINRICHS

Content Adviser: Maria Concepcion, M.S.,
Latin American and Caribbean Studies, New York University

Social Science Adviser: Professor Sherry L. Field, Department of Curriculum and Instruction,
College of Education, The University of Texas at Austin

Reading Adviser: Dr. Linda D. Labbo, Department of Reading Education,
College of Education, The University of Georgia

COMPASS POINT BOOKS
MINNEAPOLIS, MINNESOTA

Compass Point Books
3722 West 50th Street, #115
Minneapolis, MN 55410

Visit Compass Point Books on the Internet at *www.compasspointbooks.com* or
e-mail your request to *custserv@compasspointbooks.com*

Photographs ©: North Wind Picture Archives, cover, back cover (background), 1, 8, 15, 17, 29,
30, 31, 33, 34, 36, 39, 40, 46-47 (background); Stock Montage, 2 (background), 14, 19, 21, 27;
Hulton Getty/Archive Photos, 4, 9, 18, 20, 23, 25, 28, 35, 38, 41; Paul Almasy/Corbis, 5, 10; Tom
Bean/Corbis, 7; Corbis, 11; Photri-Microstock/Brent Winebrenner, 12; Dave G. Houser/Corbis,
13; Giraudon/Art Resource, N.Y., 16; PhotoDisc, 22, 26; William A. Bake/Corbis, 37.

Editors: E. Russell Primm, Emily J. Dolbear, and Melissa McDaniel
Photo Researchers: Svetlana Zhurkina and Jo Miller
Photo Selector: Catherine Neitge
Designer: Design Lab
Cartographer: XNR Productions, Inc.

Library of Congress Cataloging-in-Publication Data
Heinrichs, Ann.
   De Soto : Hernando de Soto explores the Southeast / by Ann Heinrichs.
     p. cm. — (Exploring the world)
   Includes bibliographical references and index.
   Summary: A biography of the sixteenth-century Spaniard who explored Florida and other south-
ern states, and became the first white man to cross the Mississippi River.
   ISBN 0-7565-0179-2
   1. Soto, Hernando de, ca. 1500–1542—Juvenile literature. 2. Explorers—America—Biography—
Juvenile literature. 3. Explorers—Spain—Biography—Juvenile literature. 4. America—Discovery and
exploration—Spanish—Juvenile literature. 5. Southern States—Discovery and exploration—
Spanish—Juvenile literature. [1. Soto, Hernando de, ca. 1500–1542. 2. Explorers.] I. Title. II. Series.
   E125.S7 H45 2002
   970.01'6'092—dc21   2001004730

© 2002 by Compass Point Books

Printed in the United States of America.

Table of Contents

Growing Up with a Dream

Even as a boy, Hernando de Soto knew he would have to leave home someday. When his parents died, his older brother, Juan, would inherit everything they owned. That was the law of the land in Spain. Younger sons like Hernando got nothing.

Hernando de Soto was the first European to reach the mighty Mississippi River by land.

Like other boys of that time, Hernando probably dreamed of becoming a knight. He could never have imagined what his future really held, though. Hernando would grow up to fight his way through the Americas. He would become wealthy beyond his wildest dreams. And he would come upon a mighty river—bigger than any in Europe.

Hernando de Soto was born in 1500 in southwestern Spain. It was a harsh, rocky region with dry, dusty fields. But there was something special about this part of Spain. It produced some of Spain's greatest explorers— men such as Francisco Pizarro,

De Soto and other famous explorers were born in the Extremadura region of western Spain.

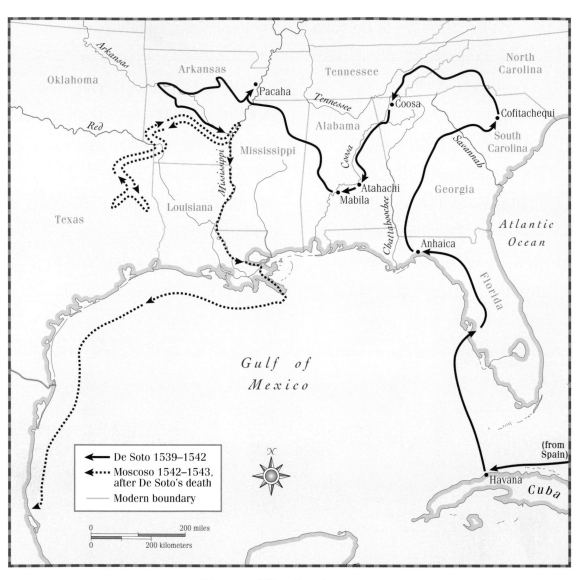

A map of De Soto's journey

Hernán Cortés, and Vasco Núñez de Balboa.

Hernando's father was a nobleman. His mother was a noblewoman from nearby Badajoz. Besides Hernando and Juan, the couple had two daughters, Catalina and Maria. They lived in Jérez de los Caballeros, a busy market town. High stone walls surrounded the town to keep out wild animals and robbers. Inside the walls, the narrow, winding streets were lined with houses and shops.

On market days, the streets of Jérez were filled with exciting sights and sounds. Salespeople shouted from their stalls.

The market was jammed with farm animals, shoppers, and children. Wandering musicians strolled among the crowds, singing songs of love and daring heroes.

A statue of the conquistador Pizarro stands in Trujillo in the Extremadura region of Spain.

Hernando could easily picture himself as such a hero. The Moors—Arab people of the Islamic faith—had invaded Spain in 711. Since then, many young Spaniards dreamed of becoming knights and driving out the Moors. Hernando was proud that some of his own relatives had fought the Moors.

With the Moors' defeat in 1492, Spain was at peace for the first time in almost eight hundred years. Now young men had to look elsewhere for adventure.

The year 1492 brought another important event. Christopher Columbus sailed west from Spain across the Atlantic Ocean. He hoped to find the Indies. These were Asian lands

Moors at prayer in Cordova, Spain

where spices, silk, pearls, and other treasures could be found. Instead, he came upon a whole "new world"—the Americas.

He did not find the Indies, but Columbus called the people who lived there "Indians" anyway. Some parts of the region had rich soil. And some parts had gold! Here, at last, was a place where young men could earn fame and fortune.

One fleet of ships after another left Spain for the Americas. Their leaders were known as the **conquistadors**. These men conquered much of Mexico, Central America, and South America. It's sometimes said that the conquistadors went to

Christopher Columbus's landing in the Americas is shown in this nineteenth-century engraving by Nathaniel Currier.

the Americas for God, glory, and gold. The priests who traveled with the conquistadors hoped to convince the Indians to become Christians. But for the conquistadors, the prize was glory and gold.

When Hernando was about fourteen years old, his father sent him to the busy city of Seville on the Guadalquivir River. Many ships took off for the Americas from Seville because the river was very deep there. Hernando was to sail with a man named Pedro Árias Dávila, who was also known as Pedrarias.

A twentieth-century view of Seville

Off to the Americas

Seville was the biggest city that young Hernando had ever seen. Down at the waterfront, men were loading ships with food, water, tools, and weapons.

Hernando found Pedrarias and gave him a letter from his father. The old man may have seemed a little scary to Hernando. He was known for

Seville's harbor was pictured in a 1594 book.

being very strict—and even cruel—to those who worked for him. But Pedrarias was one of the Spanish king's most trusted leaders.

Pedrarias welcomed Hernando and put him to work right away. The ships at the waterfront were loading up to sail to the **colony** of Darién—now the Central American country of Panama. Pedrarias was going to be the new governor there.

As dawn broke on April 11, 1514, the grand fleet of twenty ships set sail from Seville carrying more than two thousand people. Hernando could hear trumpets blaring a glorious farewell from the shore. At last, the ships

A beach in Panama today

A replica of Columbus's ship was anchored in Seville's harbor in 1992. Columbus sailed west from Spain twenty-two years before De Soto's departure.

sailed through the river's mouth into the vast Atlantic Ocean. From there, they would sail across the Atlantic Ocean. It would be twenty-two years before Hernando saw Spain again.

Hernando must have been proud to be going on this journey. Everyone in his hometown had heard of Darién. The man who started the colony, Vasco Núñez de Balboa, had also grown up in Jérez de los Caballeros. Only one year earlier, Balboa had crossed the **Isthmus** of Panama, the narrow strip of land that separates the Atlantic and Pacific Oceans. Balboa was the first European to look upon the Pacific.

Vasco Núñez de Balboa

After almost two months of sailing, the fleet came to the Caribbean island of Dominica. Here, Hernando learned just how cruel

Pedrarias could be. While their ships were being repaired, some sailors wandered off and got drunk. One refused to come aboard when it was time to leave, so Pedrarias had the man hanged. Clearly, Pedrarias was a man to be obeyed— and feared.

At last the fleet sailed into a bay at Darién. Balboa had been running the colony fairly and peacefully.

Pedrarias was a cruel man.

The Indians welcomed him wherever he went and gave him many gifts. Hernando admired Balboa, and the two became friends. But Pedrarias ruined the peace. His men stormed through one Indian village after another. They stole whatever they could and killed any Indian who stood in their way.

This sixteenth-century drawing by Flemish illustrator Theodore de Bry depicts Indians carrying gold to Balboa.

Pedrarias must have liked Hernando, because he sent the young man on many missions. Hernando saw for himself how the Spaniards raided and killed the Indians. The natives had little defense against the Spaniards' swords and guns.

By 1521, Hernando had become Captain de Soto. In 1524, the young captain took part in the **conquest** of Nicaragua. Next, he explored El Salvador and Honduras. The following year, Pedrarias put De Soto in command of an army in Nicaragua.

As a reward for his services, De Soto was given a large piece of land. Along with the land came the right to use local Indians as slaves. De Soto and a partner ran a gold mine and were involved in the slave trade.

By this time, De

Hernando de Soto

Soto was a wealthy man living a comfortable life. Yet he wanted more. Everyone knew of Hernán Cortés, the man who had stolen great riches from the Aztec Indians in Mexico. Now there was talk that the Inca Empire in Peru also had gold. And De Soto knew the man who planned to find it—Francisco Pizarro.

This engraving depicts Cortés meeting Aztec leader Montezuma in Mexico City.

The Conquest of Peru

Francisco Pizarro had been a pig farmer as a young man back in Spain, but he had come a long way since then. Pizarro was a soldier in Darién. His cruelty had made him successful there. Now he wanted to head south, to the Inca Empire.

Stretching down

Francisco Pizarro

South America's west coast, the Inca Empire was five times the size of Spain. About 6 million people lived there. The Inca had highways, bridges, and farms. Inca craft workers carved huge stones and fitted them together perfectly to make buildings. Gold, silver, and copper were dug from Incan mines. Each Incan city had a great Temple of the Sun dedicated to the sun god. But the Spaniards cared only about the gold.

Pizarro asked De Soto to join him in his conquest of the Incas, but the younger man was afraid. Pedrarias had ordered them not

Incas gathered for a ceremony to honor the Sun.

to go. If anyone was to steal the Inca riches, it was to be Pedrarias. Out of jealousy and greed, the old man had even killed Balboa. Then, in 1531, Pedrarias died. Pizarro no longer had any reason to wait. The conquest of Peru began at once.

De Soto was in charge of Pizarro's horse-men. From the coast, they marched up the rocky foothills of the Andes Mountains. Misty clouds swirled around them. Far below in the valleys,

Pizarro's men and horses marched along rocky paths in the Andes.

strange beasts called llamas grazed like sheep. The Spaniards were heading for the city of

The ruined city of Machu Picchu lies high in the Peruvian Andes. Some Incas may have escaped the Spanish invaders by fleeing to Machu Picchu, but it is not known for sure. The ancient city was rediscovered in 1911.

Cajamarca. There they would meet the Inca **emperor** Atahualpa, who was called the Sun King.

On the way, they passed through the city of Cajas. Its chief treated them well and gave them food. But De Soto repaid that kindness with cruelty. Five hundred religious women lived in the city's

Temple of the Sun. De Soto forced them outside and divided them up among his men. Enraged Inca warriors gathered to attack, but the Spaniards killed them all. Clearly, over the years De Soto had learned how to behave like a conquistador.

The Spaniards continued on. At last, they gazed down into a valley at the city of Cajamarca. Pizarro sent De Soto to meet the Incan leader. He would be the first European ever to meet the Sun King.

Atahualpa's nobles were clothed in dazzling robes decorated with gold and pearls. The emperor himself was about De Soto's age. He sat on a stool wearing a simple red wool head-dress. De Soto rode so close to him that his horse's hot breath blew in the emperor's face. De Soto made a fine speech, but Atahualpa never even looked up. Finally Atahualpa listed the Spaniards' many crimes. His spies had told him everything.

De Soto saw that Atahualpa was admiring the Spaniards' horses. De Soto decided to impress the emperor. He made his horse prance, leap, and whirl in circles. Atahualpa seemed to enjoy the tricks. Hernando began to like the man.

But Pizarro had a cunning plan. He invited Atahualpa to dinner. When the Sun King arrived, a priest demanded that he become a Christian. Then he handed Atahualpa a Bible. The emperor took one look and tossed it on the ground. That was enough for the Spaniards to attack. Spanish soldiers rushed out from all sides. All through the night the fighting went on. By morning, more than five thousand Inca lay dead.

Pizarro took Atahualpa prisoner. He promised the Inca that he would free the emperor if they brought him riches. Pack animals carrying silver and gold objects arrived from all over the empire. In all, Pizarro collected more than 11 tons of **precious** goods. Then he had emperor Atahualpa killed.

De Soto was enraged at what Pizarro did. He had become friends with Atahualpa and

Pizarro had Atahualpa murdered even after receiving a huge ransom in exchange for his release.

respected him. Still, he kept doing what he was told. He was the first European to enter Cuzco, the capital city of the Inca. Cuzco's golden Temple of the Sun was an amazing sight. But De Soto's job was to conquer. He attacked the city and left with a fortune in gold. In time, De Soto grew tired of Pizarro's leadership. In 1535, he sailed back to Spain—a wealthy man.

De Soto was the first European to enter the Inca capital city of Cuzco, shown here as it looks today.

An Empire of His Own

In Spain, De Soto was hailed as a hero. In 1536, he married Isabella de Bobadilla, Pedrarias's daughter. But life in Spain was boring compared to life in the Americas. De Soto missed the adventure. In 1537, King Charles of Spain made him governor of the Caribbean island of Cuba. King Charles also told him to set up a Spanish colony in Florida. This would not be easy. Several Spaniards had tried and failed to conquer Florida. The Indians there shot Juan Ponce de León in 1521, and he

King Charles of Spain

died of the wound. And when Pánfilo de Narváez tried to conquer Florida, only four of his men survived. But De Soto was determined. He had heard that Florida had riches as great as those of Mexico and Peru. This was his chance to conquer an empire, just as Cortés and Pizarro had.

More than six hundred men went to Florida with De Soto. They brought along horses and dogs, and hundreds of pigs for food. After sailing across the Atlantic, De Soto's ships stopped at Cuba for supplies. Then they headed for Florida. On May 25, 1539, De Soto stepped ashore south of what is now Tampa Bay.

De Soto and his men camped along Tampa Bay.

De Soto and his men traveled deep into the swamps and forests of central Florida. The hot sun beat down upon them, and the air was thick and wet. Alligators crept through the swamps, and flamingos rose up here and there in a blaze of pink. What a sight De Soto's expedition must have been! Soldiers in armor rode on horseback. Squealing pigs ran this way and that. Servants, cooks, craftsmen, and priests were followed by Indian slaves carrying supplies.

De Soto's search took the group deep into the swamps and forests of Florida.

The Indian queen gave De Soto many gifts.

When winter came, De Soto's men stayed in an Apalachee Indian village called Anhaica. Today, this is the site of Tallahassee, Florida. In the spring, they pushed north through what is now Georgia. In South Carolina, they entered a kingdom called Cofitachequi. Its chief was a beautiful woman. Hundreds of houses lined the streets of her royal city, while a grand temple stood high on a mound. The queen greeted De Soto warmly. She gave him many gifts, including long strings of pearls. The pearls had come from oysters in a nearby river.

The Spaniards begged De Soto to settle down and build the colony here. But there was no gold, so De Soto moved on. He took the queen prisoner so that the people in her villages would give him food. Later, she managed to escape. De Soto marched on through the lush mountains and forests of North Carolina and Tennessee.

De Soto took Indians prisoner as his group marched through the South.

In northwest Georgia, the men entered the empire of Coosa. This may have been the largest Indian empire in the American South. Its chief was carried on a throne to greet De Soto. He wore a fur cloak and a crown of feathers. De Soto took him prisoner. For another three months he marched through Coosa, demanding food and slaves. Again, the Spaniards begged De Soto to stop and build his colony. The soil was rich. The fields were ripe with fruits, vegetables, and grain. Spanish settlers could bring their families here and live well. But again, De Soto wanted only gold.

The Spaniards headed south through Alabama. There they met Tuscaloosa, the chief of the Choctaw people. Tuscaloosa invited De Soto into the town of Mabila (near what is now Mobile, Alabama). The Spaniards welcomed this chance to relax. Meanwhile, Tuscaloosa gathered his warriors together.

Soon, one of the bloodiest battles of the era began. Even women and children joined the fight. De Soto won the battle by setting the town on fire. In the end, hundreds of Indians were killed. Even the streams flowed with blood.

*Theodore de Bry drew this picture of a typical
Indian village such as those visited by De Soto.*

The Last Adventure

As winter fell, De Soto marched his tired men through Mississippi. Clothes, supplies, and the pearls of Cofitachequi had been destroyed at Mabila. Many of his men were wounded,

De Soto lost many men before he reached the Mississippi.

*This nineteenth-century Currier and Ives print depicts
De Soto and his followers reaching the Mississippi River.*

and others ran away. Those who were left barely survived the snowy winter.

On May 8, 1541, De Soto's men reached the widest river they had ever seen—the mighty Mississippi. It is often said that De Soto "discovered" the

Mississippi River. But other explorers had seen the mouth of the river years earlier. Spaniards had already named it *Río del Espíritu Santo*—meaning "River of the Holy Spirit." De Soto just happened to be the first European known to have reached it by land.

De Soto had no idea that he had come across the largest river in North America. To him, the river was simply annoying. It was in his way. His men spent a month building rafts to cross it. Meanwhile, Indian warriors kept sailing by in large canoes. The warriors were well trained

Indians traveled on the Mississippi River in large canoes.

De Soto and his men wandered through the forests of present-day Arkansas.

and well dressed. The Spaniards thought the empire of gold must surcly be near.

De Soto and his men crossed the Mississippi River into Arkansas. Indians there told of gold in a nearby kingdom called Pacaha. De Soto rushed to Pacaha and found furs, beads, seashells, and beautiful pottery. He sent scouts in all directions to look for gold, but they found nothing.

At this point, De Soto was not sure what to do. He wandered through the swamps and forests of Arkansas and into the foothills of the Ozark Mountains. His scouts searched west into Oklahoma. But the flat plains

Famous nineteenth-century painter Frederic Remington depicted De Soto and his conquistadors marching through the South.

there seemed an unlikely location for a great, golden empire.

In the autumn, De Soto turned south toward Louisiana. More of his men had run away, and the rest were weak or sick. By winter, De Soto himself was sick with a fever. By spring, he knew he was going to die. He decided that Luis de Moscoso would take over as leader of the group. De Soto died on May 21,

1542, near the banks of the Mississippi. No one knows exactly where. Some say it was near Arkansas City, Arkansas; others suggest Faraday, Louisiana.

De Soto had told the Indians that he would never die. Now Moscoso was afraid that if the Indians found out De Soto was dead, they would kill the remaining Spaniards. So De Soto's men hid his body for a few days. Then, in the dark of night, they put his body in a dugout log and weighed it down. They shoved the log into the Mississippi, where it sank below the swirling waters.

Only about three hundred Spaniards were left in the group

De Soto's men sank his body in the Mississippi River.

After their leader's death, De Soto's men sailed to Mexico.

now—fewer than half of those who began. Under Moscoso, they wandered through Arkansas, Texas, and Louisiana. Finally they reached the Mississippi again. They built rafts, floated down to the Gulf of Mexico, and sailed on to Mexico. People were shocked to see them. Everyone had thought they were all dead.

Hernando de Soto explored a land filled with Indians and towns. A century later, the French explored the same region. They found it almost empty. Where did all the people go? Some died in warfare. But the biggest killers were diseases from Europe. The Spaniards brought smallpox, measles, and flu to the Americas. The Indians had no **immunity** against these diseases. As a result, thousands of Indians died.

De Soto's expedition failed to start a colony in Florida. De Soto himself became too greedy to be a good leader. But at least one good thing came out of the trip. A few men who survived it reported what they had seen. Their reports tell us how Indians lived in the American South before they lost their land forever.

A sixteenth-century map depicts an Indian village in Florida.

Glossary

colony a territory settled by people from another country and controlled by that country

conquest the act of conquering

conquistadors leaders in the Spanish conquest of the Americas

emperor the leader of an empire, which is a group of countries

immunity ability to resist infection by germs

isthmus a narrow strip of land that connects two larger areas of land and lies between two bodies of water

precious having great value

Did You Know?

- Hernando de Soto and his men were the first Europeans to explore the southeastern United States.

- De Soto's expedition lasted almost four years and covered more than 4,000 miles (6,436 kilometers).

- De Soto and his men traveled with more than two hundred horses.

- Three of De Soto's assistants wrote books about the expedition. These stories are the oldest written records of life in North America.

- The Spanish soldiers used vicious dogs that were specially trained to disembowel people. That means they ripped open someone's stomach with their sharp teeth and tore out their insides.

Important Dates in De Soto's Life

1500
Hernando de Soto born in Jérez de los Caballeros, Spain

1513
Balboa becomes the first European to see the Pacific Ocean

1514
De Soto sails to Darién (Panama) with Pedrarias

1524
De Soto takes part in the conquest of Nicaragua

1531
Pizarro and De Soto begin the conquest of Peru

1539
De Soto begins exploring the southeastern United States

1541
De Soto reaches the Mississippi River

1542
De Soto dies of a fever

Important People

VASCO NÚÑEZ DE BALBOA (1475–1519) first European to look upon the Pacific Ocean

CHARLES I (1500–1558) king of Spain, and Holy Roman Emperor (as Charles V)

CHRISTOPHER COLUMBUS (1451–1506) explorer who first reached the Americas in 1492

HERNÁN CORTÉS (1485–1547) conqueror of Mexico's Aztec Empire

PEDRO ÁRIAS DÁVILA (PEDRARIAS) (1440–1531) Spanish governor of Panama and Nicaragua

JUAN PONCE DE LEÓN (1460?–1521) first Spanish explorer to reach Florida

FRANCISCO PIZARRO (1475?–1541) conqueror of the Inca Empire of Peru

Want to Know More?

At the Library

Gallagher, Jim. *Hernando de Soto and the Exploration of Florida.* Broomall,
Penn.: Chelsea House, 2001.

Larkin, Tanya. *Hernando de Soto.* New York: PowerKids Press, 2000.

Whitman, Sylvia. *Hernando de Soto and the Explorers of the American South.*
Broomall, Penn.: Chelsea House, 1991.

On the Web

**Conquest of America by Hernando de Soto
and Cabeza de Vaca**

http://www.floridahistory.com/inset11.html

Traces the footsteps of Spanish explorers such as Hernando de Soto, with
interesting links to Native American cultures

DiscoverySchool.com: Hernando de Soto

http://school.discovery.com/homeworkhelp/worldbook/atozhistory/d/155920.html

For more information about De Soto's expeditions in North and South America

Through the Mail

De Soto National Memorial
P.O. Box 15390
75th Street N.W.
Bradenton, FL 34280
941/792-0458
For more information about De Soto's journey,
as well as Native American and Spanish culture

On the Road

Parkin Archaeological State Park
P.O. Box 1110
Highways 64 and 184
Parkin, AR 72373
870/755-2500

To visit the village of Casqui, which De Soto explored
during the summer of 1541

Index

About the Author

Ann Heinrichs grew up in Fort Smith, Arkansas. She began playing the
piano at age three and thought she would grow up to be a pianist.
Instead, she became a writer. Now she has written more than fifty
books for children and young adults. Several of her books have won
national awards. Ms. Heinrichs now lives in Chicago, Illinois. She
enjoys martial arts and traveling to faraway countries.